OBLATION

Meditations on St. Benedict's Rule

OBLATION

Meditations on St. Benedict's Rule

Rachel M. Srubas

Oblation: Meditations on St. Benedict's Rule

2006 First Printing

ISBN 1-55725-488-5

Quotations from The Rule of St. Benedict are taken from *Saint Benedict's Rule: A New Translation for Today* translated by Patrick Barry, OSB. Copyright 1997 by Ampleforth Abbey Trustees. Used by permission.

Selected meditations from *Oblation* appeared previously, in a slightly different form, in the following periodicals, the editors of which the author gratefully acknowledges:

"The Humbling Rungs," "The Curve of Time," "Refectory Gestures," "A Place In the Cloister," "All Believers," "At The Feet of Teachers," and "To Receive and Reflect" in *Spirit & Life*.

"Honor Each Soul," "Your Paradoxical Gospel," "No Objection," "The Crux," and "This Is My Body" in *Benedictines Magazine* 58:1, 2005.

Library of Congress Cataloging–in–Publication Data

Srubas, Rachel M.

Oblation : meditations on St Benedict's Rule / by Rachel M. Srubas.

p. cm.

ISBN 1–55725–488-5

1. Benedict, Saint, Abbot of Monte Cassino. Regula—Meditations. 2. Devotional calendars. I. Title.

BX3004.Z5S67 2006

255'.106—dc22 2005027867

10 9 8 7 6 5 4 3 2 1

Published by Paraclete Press
Brewster, Massachusetts
www.paracletepress.com

Printed in the United States of America

DEDICATION

For my husband, Ken,

whose love for me keeps open the ear of my heart

CONTENTS

PREFACE

One summer afternoon in the early 1990s, my husband, Ken, and I risked our car's undercarriage to drive ten miles down an unpaved mountain road. Bordered on one side by sagebrush and mesas, on the other by a cliff that dropped down to the Chama River, the road led to Christ in the Desert Monastery of Abiquiu, New Mexico. Brother Aelred, a chatty monk with unforgettably bushy eyebrows, greeted us enthusiastically and welcomed us to explore the rocky, sun-baked grounds. Tiny fragrant flowers—chamomile, I think—lined the walk to the adobe chapel. There, a statue of John the Baptist, rough-hewn from a fallen tree trunk, stood behind the denim-robed Benedictine Brother who welcomed us to chant the afternoon's liturgy with his community.

A few years later, I sat in the living room of our apartment in Chicago's "Little Italy," reading a book by a not-yet-best-selling author named Kathleen Norris. She described herself as a writer who had come to Christian faith by way of an adult return to the Presbyterianism of her childhood. She also recounted how she had come to embrace the monastic wisdom of her Benedictine neighbors. Kathleen's spiritual search reminded me a little of my own.

During my college years as a student of creative writing, I had been baptized in an urban Presbyterian church whose generally activist members encouraged my contemplative development. I had eventually gone on to theological seminary, where I learned much about biblical exegesis and systematic theology, but too little, I felt, about prayer. Hungry for spiritual food, I looked up "monasteries" in

Chicago's yellow pages, and to my astonishment, found a Benedictine community on the city's south side. During that year's Advent season, in a dark, unheated chapel spiced by incense, I prayed the haunting liturgy of the hours with a half dozen monastic men and women, and my interest in their way of life deepened.

Meanwhile, as I fulfilled the academic and ecclesial requirements for ordained ministry in the Presbyterian Church (USA), I embarked on a quest to integrate my yearning for God and my passion for writing. I studied with the respected hymnist Ruth Duck. I concluded my term papers with written prayers, some of which were later published in theological journals. Inspired by what I had learned from books about the Benedictine practice of *lectio divina* (divine reading), I named my expressive, devotional discipline *scriptio divina* (divine writing), and presented a paper on this method at an academic conference on faith and writing.

Eventually, Ken and I moved to Tucson, Arizona, where my ordination to the ministry of Word and Sacrament coincided more or less with my official entry into Benedictine spirituality. At the heart of this desert city sits the monastery of the Benedictine Sisters of Perpetual Adoration. The monastery is a striking tile-roofed structure with palm trees in front and an orange grove in back, next to a former tennis court now painted with a seven-circuit labyrinth. The monastery's serene, spacious chapel is open about twelve hours per day to the public, for whom liturgy books are provided for lauds and vespers (morning and evening prayers). Once per month, about fifty oblates (an ecumenical array of non-monastic associates of the monastery), meet to find support and insight for their practice of Benedictine spirituality.

I joined the oblate community and developed a warm friendship with their energetic Director, Sister Lenora Black, OSB. Her sisters in the monastery's Liturgical Vestments Department tailored the alb I wore at my ordination. Sister Lenora wore her best black suit to my ordination service, read publicly from the Bible during the liturgy, and happily snapped pictures afterward. Since then, I've gone through more than one transition in my ministry, but true to their vow of stability, the Benedictines have remained a constant though dynamic community that welcomes me to make myself at home in their midst. I've been blessed many times over by Benedictine hospitality, good humor, and guidance, and have gratefully claimed my place among centuries of spiritual seekers for whom Saint Benedict brilliantly distills the practical wisdom of the Christian gospel.

This diary of Benedictine prayers is one person's response to St. Benedict's Rule, a fifteen-hundred-year-old guide to faithful living in community. Much in the Rule, ancient though it is, pertains to the contemporary spiritual practices of prayer, humility, study, work, hospitality, and simplicity. Numerous present-day Christian writers (and a few Buddhists, too) have popularized interest in Benedictine wisdom. The works of Joan Chittister, Norvene Vest, Esther de Waal, John McQuiston and David Steindl-Rast, to name just a few authors of Benedictine books, swell bookstores' spirituality sections.

I pray that this slender book of prayers inspired by passages from most every chapter of St. Benedict's Rule will encourage readers to explore the Rule for themselves. I give thanks for Abbot Patrick Barry's lucid, inclusive English translation of the Rule, from which I quote amply in these pages. Every one of the prayers to follow is an oblation, an offering to God. The prayers are personal, yet also intended to speak meaningfully to readers' own dilemmas and aspirations in light of the unfailing faithfulness of God, best known to us in Christ.

INTRODUCTION

Benedictine Spirituality and the Writing Life

To the Beginning

This morning I was a little late for lauds. Other than the sisters chanting in their choir stalls, the only person present for the liturgy was a man I often see in the monastery chapel. He sits in a front pew, holding an open Bible close to his face and squinting as though he is terribly near-sighted and really interested in what the Bible says. I made my way down the center aisle, bowed, turned the pages of a liturgy book, and found my place in Psalm 57. With the sisters, I chanted, "My heart is faithful, O God, my heart is faithful."

More than that could be said of my complicated heart. Thanks to these sisters, and to God and St. Benedict, I have a community with whom I'm free to pray my heart out and find rest for my soul. Not to mention breakfast for my body. After Lauds ended, I gratefully joined my friend Sister Lenora for coffee and a slice of homemade banana bread in the monastery dining room. She handed me the keys to Monte Cassino, the second story guest apartment named after Saint Benedict's mountaintop monastery in Italy. (The basement guest apartment is called "Subiaco," after St. Benedict's cave.) My plan was to do just what I'm doing: to sit in the quiet solitude of Monte Cassino and write.

I had brought with me a companion, of sorts, a thumb-sized raven carved from onyx by a Zuni artisan. Two tiny inlaid turquoise eyes suggest that the bird is as watchful a raven as the one that often appears in icons of St. Benedict. According to Saint Gregory's account, that raven squawked and flapped away with poisoned bread in its beak, saving St. Benedict from the malice of an envious rival who had sent it to the saint. The name that St. Benedict gave his raven is not known, so when Lenora showed my carved raven to the sisters at the next breakfast table, I told them, "He needs a name." Without missing a beat, Sister Joan Therese said, "Quoth." And so it is. Quoth, the raven, watches over me as I write, as I remember how I got here, to Monte Cassino, and to the beginning of this Benedictine book.

Prayerful Reading, Prayerful Writing

In the Preface, I retraced briefly my formation in the spirituality of St. Benedict. In this Introduction, I'll flesh out some of the details of that development, with two purposes in mind. First, for readers of the prayers that follow, some knowledge of their author may be helpful for establishing their context and easing their accessibility. Second, by recollecting in this Introduction how I have appropriated and adapted aspects of Benedictine spirituality, I hope to acquaint readers who may be new to this fifteen-hundred-year-old tradition with one of its hallmarks: the practice of *lectio divina* (prayerful reading). Before I reflect on my personal experience of lectio divina, let me comment more generally on Benedict's instructions concerning lectio, and on its modern developments.

Benedict advocates for balance in the Christian life. In addition to the *Opus Dei* (the Liturgy of the Hours, also called the divine office or the work of God), part of the day is to be devoted to manual labor, and another part to lectio divina. Many contemporary people of faith are drawn to

Benedict because his teachings not only offer an antidote to the culture of overwork, they also promote an approach to sacred reading that engages the whole person, and not only the rational intellect. Practitioners of lectio divina read short passages of Scripture or other holy texts in a meditative spirit, alert to hear God speaking to them through the text. Lectio involves emotion and imagination more than analysis. Traditionally, the lectio process is thought to promote the individual's solitary, devotional immersion in the implications of a sacred text, to the point at which verbalized, internal prayer ultimately gives way to contemplative silence.

Growing numbers of Christians interested in strengthening their inner life are participating in groups that practice lectio divina collectively. While such gatherings are interspersed by silence, they also invite participants to speak in response to the Holy Spirit's prompting, as experienced through a shared holy reading. Rather than culminating in a wordless communion with God, group lectio invites practitioners to name the practical intentions they feel moved by the Spirit to carry out in the coming days.

Another variation on lectio divina is a process that I have called *scriptio divina,* or prayerful writing (religion professor Stephanie Paulsell has also employed the term scriptio divina in a scholarly context). As a spiritual practice, scriptio divina begins with the open-hearted reading of Scripture or another spiritual text, but the prayer that emerges, neither tacit nor spoken, is written. Writing prompted by the Spirit who speaks through Scripture may result in prayers addressed to God such as those that comprise this book. Or, the scriptio divina process may lead to writing that lacks the formal conventions of prayer but is nevertheless devotional in origin. In the remainder of this Introduction, I'll reflect on my personal experiences of lectio divina and scriptio divina, in solitude and in community.

As I Write, I Pray

Looking back on my formation in Benedictine spirituality, I can't separate my discovery of lectio divina from my practice of prayerful writing. The two developments happened more or less simultaneously, about eight years after I'd been baptized, when I devoted a summer to composing a sequence of prayers inspired by the lectionary texts for that year's Advent season. While it was still a work in progress, I sent the manuscript to the members of a writers' group I had co-founded. In an accompanying letter, I described my writing process in terms more Benedictine than I realized at the time: "I've written every poem . . . by reading the lectionary passage, open to whatever verse or verses particularly shimmer for me, and in the hope that the poem might open the biblical text in a new way to its, and the poem's, reader." My pastor, the Reverend Jeff Doane, and the worship committee of Lincoln Park Presbyterian Church in Chicago, arranged to have 200 copies of my completed Advent manuscript photocopied with a sturdy lavender cardstock cover bearing the title *In This Meantime*. The members of the congregation each received a copy of the booklet, from which I read publicly during Advent worship services that year. It would be difficult to find a more nurturing community for a writer of faith than Lincoln Park Presbyterian Church. I thank that congregation for blessing my creative, contemplative development.

As is the case with this book, the introduction to *In This Meantime* was the last part of it to be written, and by that time, I had begun to articulate the kinship between my writing life and lectio divina. *In This Meantime*'s introduction explained, "each poem functioned for me, while I wrote it, as a kind of lectio divina. This, according to Richard J. Foster . . . is a way of reading the Bible in which 'our task is not so much to study the passage as to be initiated into the reality of which it speaks.'" That a Quaker (Foster) introduced me, a Presbyterian, to lectio divina, testifies to the ecumenical appeal of the practice.

The following spring, at Calvin College's Festival of Faith and Writing, I presented a paper called "*Scriptio Divina*: A Poetics of Prayer." Today that title strikes me as mildly pretentious, but it certainly was an earnest effort to name the relationship between Benedictine scriptural prayer and the creative writing process. Thelma Hall's book *Too Deep For Words: Rediscovering Lectio Divina,* was a helpfully provocative resource for me. In a presentation accessible to contemporary readers with no background in monastic studies, Hall describes lectio's fluid, intuitive movement as a means for discerning God's personalized address to the individual practitioner. To a literary artist with a mystical bent like me, this sounded great. It was thrilling to imagine that the Holy Spirit would speak to me directly through biblical texts, and lead me to write my own prayers.

But that leap—from lectio divina to scriptio divina—from divine reading to divine writing—meant that I had departed from the classical contemplative tradition of the West, and failed to reach, some would say, the profound communion with God possible only through unspoken devotion. "Contemplation," I told the audience at Calvin College, "is a passive, silent prayer, an experience of love between the person and God, which Thelma Hall describes as 'too deep for words.'" Too deep for words? I appreciated the reference to Romans and the Spirit who sighs on our behalf because we do not know how to pray as we ought, but I had come to believe that I ought to pray in writing before giving up on words. I trusted the Spirit to speak *through* the words I was given to write.

I was, and am, a person of faith for whom writing deepens devotion. The loving silence at the heart of my relationship with God is not broken but enriched by the language of prayer. In the basement Assembly Room of the very monastery in which I write these words, a Centering Prayer group meets for silent meditation on Monday nights. I honor their practice, but I feel more at home in the monastery's chapel, chanting psalms, or up here in Monte Cassino, where my laptop computer hums, and phrases of praise come to me, and the keyboard clicks softly at my fingertips. As I write, I pray, and Quoth, the raven, is my witness.

An Image that Shines

Vigilance is the task not only of shrewd ravens, but of human beings, too, who, like those black, observant birds that neither sow nor reap, would spontaneously spy out gifts from God, the bright bits of sustenance that keep us going throughout our lives. I am, among other things, a teacher of vigilance. Some of my students are parishioners, looking for signs of divine life. Others are students in the classes I teach on writing as a spiritual practice. It's been my privilege to help cultivate clouds of literary witnesses, communities of writers over whom a reverent hush has fallen whenever one of their members has written an image that shines with sacramental vitality. I think of the Roman Catholic priest on sabbatical who took one of my classes. When he read to us the poem he had written about his dead father's wedding ring, which he wore on his own hand, the light in the classroom turned gold.

All I had asked the priest and his classmates to do was to look—really look—at an object, and to say what they read in it, what it told them. In other words, I invited them to practice, with the stuff of their lives, lectio and scriptio divina. These prayer forms involve expectant attentiveness and patient repetition. The repeated, prayerful reading of Scripture or of any other holy thing, requires, as does careful writing, counter-cultural single-mindedness, the stillness of a raven carved from stone, and the watchfulness of its turquoise eyes. For some contemplatives, like Thelma Hall and the Centering Pray-ers in the monastery's basement, such watchful stillness is all that is needed. For others, to witness the ripple of divine life present in a centuries-old and translated text demands a response in kind, a wording of the faith that has just been quickened by the Scripture. Writers of faith give thanks that in Jesus, the Word was made flesh, but the Word has always seemed incarnate to them.

Now, having said that, let me confess: When I first began reading the Bible in my twenties, I couldn't believe how skimpy the prose was. Considering, for example, Mark's relatively spare account of Jesus' death, I could hear that creative writing workshop cliché ringing in my ears: "Show, don't tell." Where was all the detail? How was I supposed to be moved, much less converted, by so minimal a description of what could have been such a vivid narrative? (Hollywood has addressed the same question, sometimes with problematic results.) I didn't dare tell anyone at my new church that the Bible bored me; I just waited, in a state of private spiritual embarrassment, to feel some passion about the Passion, or about the life that preceded it.

This is where Saint Ignatius, who lived in the sixteenth century, a thousand years later than Benedict, helped me. Whereas the Benedictine practice of lectio divina involves interior, verbal rumination, Ignatian contemplation is more imagistic—a helpful prayer form for filmmakers, I would think, with its pictured, storytelling thrust. Not until I had learned, with the help of Ignatius, to imagine my own participation in the events of the four Gospels, was I able to appreciate those texts linguistically, and to let their words lead me to prayerful writing. I'm thankful I followed that lead, and risked sharing with friends in faith the prayers I had written. When they told me that some of my prayers had become their prayers, then I knew that even through the solitary, contemplative practice of writing, I could contribute to what the apostle Paul calls "the common good," and make an offering, an oblation, to the Christian community.

Holy Hearings

Even before 2000, when I officially became an oblate—a non-monastic affiliate of the Benedictine Sisters of Perpetual Adoration—they welcomed me to offer my writings for the common good of those served by their congregation. The sisters regularly publish my poems, prayers, and essays in their magazine, *Spirit & Life*. The magazine reaches roughly 10,000 readers, including many of the women and men who attend monthly oblates' meetings at Tucson's monastery. Insofar as their stations in life allow it, these oblates seek to live the Christian life according to the Rule of St. Benedict.

Like the Bible before it, the Rule was, for me, an initially impenetrable document. Despite its modest length, this ancient pamphlet intimidated me, and I doubted whether I would ever find it alive and meaningful. My religious education as a Presbyterian clergywoman had required me to work with original sources, many of them in Hebrew and Greek. Surely I could handle Benedict's "little rule for beginners" (as he calls it) translated from Latin into contemporary English. But still, I needed help finding my way into this ancient text, which, when I first encountered it, seemed shrouded by a medieval mystique.

One evening at The Book Stop, Tucson's comfy used bookstore next door to Santa Barbara Ice Creamery, I sat in a creaking armchair, enjoying a frozen banana and scanning the titles on the religion shelves. My eyes lighted on *The Rule of Benedict: Insights for the Ages* by Joan Chittister, and within a few minutes, I knew I'd found the help I needed. I read the book between sessions at a huge, triennial conference of Presbyterian women in Louisville, Kentucky, where I roomed with three other attendees. Our hotel happened to be very near the corner of Fourth Street and Muhammad Ali Boulevard, formerly Walnut Street. At that intersection a monument commemorates a compassionate epiphany of Thomas Merton's, perhaps the twentieth century's best-known follower of St. Benedict's Rule. The Louisville conference, including tight quarters shared by diverse personalities, turned out to be an ideal setting in which to discover Benedict's and Chittister's practical wisdom concerning life in Christian community.

Community—comprised of belonging, relationship, and service—is the experience for which, I believe, many contemporary spiritual seekers yearn. It's through the community experience of work and worship, play and prayer that unconnected individuals become united in the knowledge that they are loved by the God of Jesus, and commit to living in Christ's name. In growing numbers, non-monastic people who already belong to worshiping congregations are also drawn to monasteries. This is because the sisters and brothers invite them to share in their community and in a historic, enduring way of life that brings home to them the practicality and promise of the Christian gospel.

For those longing to listen to that gospel with the ear of the heart, the meditative yet purposeful discipline of lectio divina is incomparable. When a group of reflective souls participate together in the lectio process, the contemplative encounter with God in a sacred text expands to make room for a multiplicity of holy hearings. The hunger for such a shared encounter among Tucson's Benedictine oblates gave rise to a Saturday morning lectio group that is a safe and sacred circle largely indebted for its procedural guidelines to Benedictine oblate Norvene Vest's book *Gathered In The Word: Praying the Scripture In Small Groups*. Among the most important ground rules for the group is the gentle prohibition on cross-talk, which helps participants listen to one another without expressing judgment, or offering or seeking advice. In response to repeated readings of the day's text (which are punctuated by silence), each participant offers responses and intentions while the others listen mindfully, and resist the sometimes strong temptation to fill quiet pauses with chatter. In this way, the Saturday morning lectio group reminds me of the students in my classes on writing as a spiritual practice: At its best, each community agrees to let their busy minds and mouths be muted, so that the Spirit might speak and be heard through the Word, or through the experience of wording.

Whether I am teaching writers, preaching for worshipers, leading a prayer group, or guiding spiritual retreatants, I try to convey and encourage the lively lectio spirit, and the spirit of prayerful writing, which I believe Benedict began cultivating in me even before I knew him by name. The discipline of listening for God's word in Scripture (whether or not the listener writes in prayerful response) is essentially solitary. Just as I write these words in solitude, so did I read in solitude the Rule of St. Benedict that inspired, prayer by prayer, this book. Corporate contemplative practices, including praying and writing in groups, can foster faith communities, but community is equally strengthened by the presence of people who can stand their own company, who can sit still alone long enough to discover their divine, indwelling companion.

St. Benedict's faith was formed in the cavernous solitude of Subiaco, and his vision of faithful community life was realized on Monte Cassino. He is the quintessential hermit and abbot, a contemplative writer whose Rule is replete with the fruits of his own lectio divina. May *Oblation: Meditations on St. Benedict's Rule* offer Benedict an homage befitting such an exemplary teacher. And may this book invite its readers to read, pray, and write their own prayers, with a heart open and attuned to the living Christ whose love Benedict preferred above all else.

Within My Reach

This, then, is the beginning of my advice: make prayer the first step in anything worthwhile that you attempt. Persevere and do not weaken in that prayer. Pray with confidence, because God, in his love and forgiveness, has counted us as his own sons and daughters.

(PROLOGUE, ST. BENEDICT'S RULE)

You are here, within my reach.
All I need is to open my hands,
accept your gift to me of breath,
turn my awareness your way,
and I find you waiting for me,
patiently, closely.

I don't need to hide myself from you,
who made me in mercy
and know me completely.

When I go to you in prayer, anxiety
turns gradually to serenity.
You smooth my fear with a steady hand
until it subsides,
and I am simplified.

Freed of worry, unhindered by my history,
I need not ask for your favor,
but only for the faithfulness
to take you at your Word,
imbued by holy, emboldening Spirit.
Source of my confidence,

Purpose in my perseverance,
accept this prayer in the name of Christ,
my beginning,
my fulfillment.

I, Too, Belong

For a rule of life they have only the satisfaction of their own desires. Any precept they think up for themselves and then decide to adopt they do not hesitate to call holy. Anything they dislike they consider inadmissible.

(CHAPTER 1, ST. BENEDICT'S RULE)

Gathering God,
you fashioned me
not for isolation, but community.
As much as any member of your body,
I, too, belong
to the people you summon,
the disciples you instruct.

When I submit my shifting mind
to your wisdom, and commit my hands to your work,
my being, brimming with undirected energy,
becomes a purposeful blessing.
Yet I resist you, pursue my private wants,
squander sacred liberty on frivolities.
Time is a grace I too often waste, casually
withholding kindness, inventing excuses

to justify pointless rebellions.
For fear of becoming someone
not of my own invention, I struggle
to fend off my redemption.

Transgress my toughened skin
and loosen with your love
the arrogant knots of my self.
Transform my defiance into reliance
on you. Let me experience as true
what, deep down, I always knew:
to surrender independence
is freedom. To serve other people
is to be made whole in you.

Honor Each Soul

They should not select for special treatment any individual in the monastery. They should not love one more than another unless it is for good observance of the Rule and obedience. *(CHAPTER 2, ST. BENEDICT'S RULE)*

You prodigal, indiscriminate lover.
You came to us in Jesus,
who gave himself equally to people
who called each other enemies.
Claiming no favorites, cherishing all,
Jesus looked into the eyes
and laid his hands on anyone

deformed by disease and deemed unclean.
Yet he also embraced the priests
who barred these "impure" from the temple.
He dined with the priests' own oppressors—
the Roman occupiers
and their mercenary tax collectors.

Jesus lived a recklessly welcoming gospel
that unshackled all who could hear it
and struck fear in others whose stature would suffer
were they to practice the justice he preached.

Where do I stand in an economy of grace
that venerates no dignitaries,
denigrates no "poor slobs"?
I want to be chosen, distinguished, upheld.
I want to choose whom to invite and whom
to leave off the guest list, exclude from the table.

Still, inside me another, deeper urge persists:
the hunger of a purged, non-partisan spirit
capable of love without conditions.
It's your Spirit in me,
your Word in my body, teaching me
to honor each soul you lead into my life,
to see in each face, beautiful or ugly,
the features of the living Christ.

To Listen In Concert

To get the balance right it should be remembered that, whereas it is right for subordinates to obey their superior, it is just as important for the superior to be far-sighted and fair in administration. (CHAPTER 3, ST. BENEDICT'S RULE)

I live in a land of self-styled mavericks,
a society that venerates soloists
and emulates lonesome heroes.

Your way leads out of isolation,
multiplies me and me
into us.
You call your people
to put our heads and hearts together,
to listen in concert, consult one another
before we decide.
It would be more efficient to trust
my own instincts solely,
to horde responsibility, act unilaterally,
and sweep up the credit when it came—
so says the chatter of an only-childish brain.

You call into my awareness a world
wider than my single mind. When you speak to me
through a multiplicity of human voices,
you unsettle in me the idol of certainty
and alter my priorities.
You reach through my prayers
into my personality
to remind me you are Trinity,

the holy plural unity,
three ways of being wholly divine.

The company of the faithful welcomes me
not to demand my own way, but to coexist
with other women and men, and practice
the discipline of listening to them.

Your Paradoxical Gospel

Your hope of fulfillment should be centered in God alone.
(CHAPTER 4, ST. BENEDICT'S RULE)

Sacred Encircler, I'm far less ready
to surrender my independence
than you are to surround me with your love.

I dodge your embrace.
I busy myself, chase down achievements,
then trip on some humbling truth and stumble
into your paradoxical gospel,
a story so old, so told, I'm startled
when it confronts me with the falsity
of my frenetic efforts,
the reality of your greater mercy.
You don't hand me glory. You ask me
to empty my hands of my burdens,
my mind of my plans.

You command me to love you entirely, and others
as though they lived in my skin.
In my fear that I'll disappear
if I give in to you, I fall to the depths
of my unbelief. This inward poverty
comes with a challenge:
to give up my pretense of self-sufficiency—
or to persist in it,
and see where it gets me.

Ready Me to Respond

With a ready step inspired by obedience they respond by their action to the voice that summons them.

(CHAPTER 5, ST. BENEDICT'S RULE)

In the beginning, you sighed.
You spoke over chaos and made the original day.
This day shines as that one must have done,
the sky a bright arc,
the earth a dark dynamic,
everywhere, beings you articulate in love.
When you speak, life pulses in my limbs.
I run with wild energy you breathe into me.

Your second word comes: a summons,
curbing the frenzy, guiding my feet.
Open the ear of my heart today.
Encourage me to do a harder thing

than mere hearing;
ready me to respond.

I'm fond of my internal monologue,
the sound of my mental soliloquy,
relevant to no one but me.

Obedience. The very word fences me in.
I chafe at the thought, and then—
find myself shaken awake
by some act of uncommon decency
or outrageous violation
that shouts me out of my self-
preoccupation and back
to the land of the living:

here, where you breathe
and name everything,
where my heart's ear bends
and my life depends
first on obedient listening.

No Objection

. . . the disciple's role is to be silent and listen.

(CHAPTER 6, ST. BENEDICT'S RULE)

Jesus, when you lived among us,
traveling,
teaching on lakesides,
people thronged and clamored, eager
for the healing you had power to impart
with a word.

With your cures came commandments:
love God so fiercely
you'll love one another
as though there's no barrier
between another's suffering and your own.

I see myself on an ancient beach,
wave-tumbled rocks hard beneath my feet.
An argument sits on my tongue,
a bred-in-the-bone sense of self-preservation.

Yet for some reason, I raise
no objection to you and your foolish,
self-sacrificial compassion. I look
across the water's cold, complicated surface,
raise only a hand,
and skip a flat stone.

The Humbling Rungs

. . . our proud attempts at upward climbing really will bring us down, whereas to step downwards in humility is the way to lift our spirit up towards God.

(CHAPTER 7, ST. BENEDICT'S RULE)

From the level plain of my human-sized life,
I lift up to you my weary eyes.
I kneel amid the clutter of dashed aspirations—
inflated hopes that fell flat, upheld as they'd been
only by an air of importance,
not by the humbling rungs of true prayer.

I tried to fly on my own power. I dreamed
of the praise I would reap, the respect, the rewards.
I strove for nothing
but my culture's highest goal,
and for a moment I saw it—success, glinting gold. I flew
like a self-made god toward that sun
until my weak wings melted away,
and I plunged
to the planet I inhabit
with all the other small creatures,
the ordinary mortals who reach, as I do, for you.

Here on earth, the ground is steady underfoot,
and heaven hangs higher overhead than the sun.
Now, to bring you my bruised gratitude and petitions,
my prayers descend a ladder of confession, one-by-one.

Mystery Overcomes Me

The first step of humility is to cherish at all times the sense of awe with which we should turn to God. It should drive forgetfulness away; it should keep our minds alive to all God's commandments. (CHAPTER 7, ST. BENEDICT'S RULE)

Like health, I take you for granted.
Or like a pill to be swallowed, an antibiotic
after the symptoms of illness have gone,
I forget you until late in the day,
when my work is done.

The sun dissolves, calls it a night,
and the understudy moon goes bright.
I think I ought to stargaze,
walk to the end of the driveway
and cast my eyes skyward
to cultivate some semblance of awe.
But I'm beat, so I snap out the light.

And then the darkness,
the effortless darkness
reveals its dark secrets to me.
Mystery overcomes me,
awes me to sleep.

All My Dear Falsehoods

The second step of humility is not to love having our own way nor to delight in our own desires.

(CHAPTER 7, ST. BENEDICT'S RULE)

I am the road that will guide you to God.
I unravel lies that seduced you.
I am the life you still try to elude.
When you abandon me,
I wait for you. When you return,
I embrace you.

Some days I prefer
to ignore your assurances,
pave my own path, lose my own way,
cross quicksand if I have to—
anything but
relinquish my will.

Remember the blistering, narcissistic desert,
the devil who taunted you there?
You know it well—the desire, the drive
to conceive and control, predict and prevail.
You, too, have wrestled the egoistic impulse,
the credit-hoarding greed of spirit
that flares within and keeps me,
on some days, from offering praise,
stops me from seeking your face
or following your excellent way.

I'm left to my echoing solitude,
murmuring my own name.

Jesus, teach me to pray. Lend me your hand.
Talk to me of forgiveness until
all my dear falsehoods fall away.
Mend the cracked compass of my mind,
and guide me to my true desire.

At the Feet of Teachers

The third step of humility is to submit oneself out of love of God to whatever obedience under a superior may require of us.

(CHAPTER 7, ST. BENEDICT'S RULE)

Thank you for the ones who nurtured me
when I could only crawl,
who fell to their knees to see from my small perspective,
and upheld me when I took my first, faltering steps.
They helped me walk, however unsteadily,
in the way you had laid out for me.
When I veered toward danger, they forbade me to go any
further.

For my good, early guardians and trustworthy teachers,
who insisted I obey them when my preference for
transgression
would have put me at risk, I thank you, at last.

It took me decades to appreciate the limits they set, to understand
I'd been hemmed in, behind and before,
not by arbitrary prohibitions, but by your love.

The finest preachers do little more than remind us:
the teachings of Moses and Jesus
mandate reverence, self-control, and kindness.
For exacting instructors who embody compassion
without condescension, confidence without arrogance,
who teach me my neighbors are everyone without exception
and expect me to serve them
not as whimsical option
but as sacred obligation, I thank you.

Help me, O God, to outgrow
any remnant of defiant adolescence within me.
Show me the difference between sullen docility
and discerning obedience. Open my conscience
to prophets who speak on behalf of the silenced
and issue ultimatums grounded in your covenants.
Sit me down at the feet of teachers
who will school me in humility.

The Crux

The fourth step of humility is to . . . readily [accept] in patient and silent endurance . . . any hard and demanding thing that may come our way in the course of . . . obedience, even if they include harsh impositions which are unjust.

(CHAPTER 7, ST. BENEDICT'S RULE)

Late in his truncated life, a modern martyr said,
unearned suffering must somehow be redemptive.
At the crux of the cross, injustice meets up with endurance,
brutality with silence, violence with patience.
As long as the crucifixions continue,
and harsh impositions are borne in obedience;
until all the crosses have been dismantled
and bridges are built with their beams,
you will reclaim the lives of all who die on them
and all who don't: the masterminds,
the engineers and carpenters.

While armed peacekeepers
fight to eliminate tyrants by force,
you redeem, by death-defying grace,
even dictators who scoff in your face.
In the wild illogic of the cross,
death intersects with your tenderness
and you bring forth life irresistible: resurrection
of the least, and of the least forgivable.

The Listener I Need

The fifth step of humility is that we should not cover up but humbly confess to our superior or spiritual guide whatever evil thoughts come into our minds and the evil deeds we have done in secret.

(CHAPTER 7, ST. BENEDICT'S RULE)

Take my mistakes. Take my half-
acknowledged manipulations,
the lies I tell, the honesty withheld.
Take the little fortress I've built around myself
and break it down. My heart has gone
unheard for too long; my life
is overgrown, unwieldy. I can't—
I never could—contain it alone.

Lead me to the listener I need,
a confessor unafraid to look at me
with clear and unaverted eyes.
Send me a soul-friend, someone
kind enough to extend to me
your warm, accepting arms,
and wise enough to understand
truths in me I scarcely recognize.

Closer to Real

The sixth step of humility . . . is to accept without complaint really wretched and inadequate conditions so that when faced with a task of any kind they would think of themselves as poor workers. . . .

(CHAPTER 7, ST. BENEDICT'S RULE

Miryam was perhaps fifteen
when her uterus, firm and untried,
conceived you. Barley flatbread
enriched her blood and fed you
until the light-hungry world received you.
We know nothing of your mother's labor,
but labor, we do know, is hard.

Did a stonemason's calloused hands
wipe blood from your small, startled face?
Did he smooth sweat from Miryam's forehead,
or hold himself at arm's length, keeping
the cleanliness codes you would grow up
to break? Whatever the forgotten details
of your remarkably human emergence,
surely it was all demanding and delicate,
worrisome work, welcoming you—
a needy, naked infant—
keeping you warm and alive.

When I pity myself
for my own laborious efforts, remind me
to summon the scene of your birth.
Not the crèche of sentimental devotion,

but something closer to real: the pressure
of late pregnancy and long travel, the prospect
of burdensome taxes,
the scent of manure and fear; and then—
the restless work of breastfeeding
under a black sky, huge and unanswering,
an easterly star alarmingly near.

This Litany Forever

The seventh step of humility is that we should be ready to speak of ourselves as of less importance and less worthy than others, not as a mere phrase but we should really believe it in our hearts. Thus in a spirit of humility we make the psalmist's words our own: I am no more than a worm with no claim to be a human person for I am despised by others and cast out by my own people.

(CHAPTER 7, ST. BENEDICT'S RULE)

If the earth had turned
against me;
if gunfire had always
accompanied birdsong;
if I had survived
on what stale bread I could steal;
if my sister had not been so lucky;
if I had watched her life
drain away like sewage;
if violence had dwelt among us

like some traumatized uncle;
if I had grown up confronted by the brute
mechanisms of automatic weapons
at checkpoints on the road to my home,
or had stayed barricaded in our ancient,
occupied neighborhood, growing
familiar with blood's sticky texture;
if I could add to this litany forever
and never tell one untrue tale, then—
I would know what it is
to be considered no more
than a worm.

I would be capable of both:
deep evil, great faith.
You would gaze on me,
whisper, *my beloved,* and in secret,
you would break my chains.
I would walk
through our ruined city,
ready to die if I had to, your hand
strong and easy in mine.

To Honor These Elders

The eighth step of humility teaches us to do nothing which goes beyond what is approved and encouraged by the common rule of the monastery and the example of our seniors.
(CHAPTER 7, ST. BENEDICT'S RULE)

The image in my morning mirror
looks older than I remember. Clearly,
I've outlived my youth: the truth
of my age winks back at me.
Since when have fine lines,
the cartography of time, etched my face?
I can trace a history of smiles
from the corners of my eyes, and of worries,
preserved between my brows.

If it weren't for these creases,
who would I be? A perpetual innocent,
unmarked by history?

Embolden me, Ancient One,
not to squint-away the years,
nor to fear the shortening of the future.
Let me look into the complicated faces
of the old, and recognize enduring grace.
Inspire me to honor these elders
whose long lives are made
mostly of memory, for whom a new day
blooms, unexpected, a blessing.
When I take time for granted,
remind me I'll eventually return

to the dust from which you fashioned me.
Help me live gratefully for the time being,
this lifespan between ashes and ashes.

The Silence You Speak

The ninth step of humility leads us to refrain from unnecessary speech and to guard our silence by not speaking until we are addressed. (CHAPTER 7, ST. BENEDICT'S RULE)

In the indigo hours,

in fields where crickets comment from the reeds,

in hushed coronary chambers, the chapel inside every person,

you dwell, noiselessly telling of your mercy.

You move, as well, down intensive care corridors busy at all hours,

through hospital rooms pulsing with the glow

of television game shows and heart monitors.

Beneath city streets you uphold

innumerable hurrying feet and murmur the stories of your origins.

You wait within the muted elegance of carpeted staterooms.

Among the indistinguishable knuckles and vertebrae in mass graves,

you retrieve and reweave each disappeared life.

The silence you speak is frequently mistaken for absence.

The peace you've left with us all but surpasses our grasp.

The Slightest Provocation

The tenth step of humility teaches that we should not be given to empty laughter on every least occasion. . . .

(CHAPTER 7, ST. BENEDICT'S RULE)

I knew a woman whose voice rang out at the slightest provocation,
brassy as a school bell commanding attendance.
I knew a man whose need to amuse chafed him like wool. Twitchy,
he'd watch for a chance to pull a one-liner, seize a moment's relief
from the rash he wore, which only a big laugh could scratch.
I once knew a boy who discovered electrical power
would surge through his limbs whenever he teased other kids.
The meaner the fun, the better the buzz.

Do we ever grow up? Or do the children we were
just grow larger, subtler, more self-deceived?
These are adult questions, rooted in retrospect, tinged by
tragedy.
Once upon a time we didn't look back. There was so little
past, and the present
was sufficient—hilarious, in fact. We cracked up. We keeled
and gasped
and kept laughing until we'd forgotten what had been funny.
But you remember all that. You were there, blessing us silly.
It was your joy we reveled in. We were your children.

The Only Word I Needed

The eleventh degree of humility is concerned with the manner of speech appropriate in a monastery. We should speak gently and seriously with words that are weighty and restrained. We should be brief and reasonable in whatever we have to say and not raise our voices to insist on our own opinions. (CHAPTER 7, ST. BENEDICT'S RULE)

Long ago, before time had a name,
over the shapeless emptiness of space,
you spoke
of sunlight and midnight, mountains and oceans,
mammals and shellfish and silken-feathered birds.
By your words the world was created.
Your language—original, sculptural,
humming with meaning and melody—had power

to make human beings and teach them to live
reverently, humbly, in peace.

They half-listened to you.
Serpentine whispers also hissed in their ears.
They sank their teeth into the sticky fruit
of sweet success.
They talked with their mouths full,
stacking up stories of their accomplishments
until structural flaws caused their towers to fall
into babble and rubble.

Talking heads proffered blame,
but your poetry, burning on the lips of rare prophets,
called for the repair of the world.
Only your word, freshly breathed
into the heart of all hurt, only your wisdom,
womb-borne and tender, could strengthen
and bless the wounded, weary people.
You wandered among them,
unbound yet rabbinic, speaking a dialect
nonsensical to legalists and bureaucrats,
understandable to slaves,
sensible to women,
teachable to children and broken-down men.
This scrappy majority got wind of your mercy
and surged in from the overcrowded margins of the world
to surround you on beaches and hillsides
and hear your healing speech.

When word spread that you had said
unprecedented things about a kingdom

hidden within every person,
some wanted you dead.
They did what they wanted.
The earth went silent as a skull, primordially dark.
But deep in the marrow of your crucified bones,
a spark sputtered.
You shook off the spices and rags of death
to utter, letter by letter, the names of your beloved,
the people you had claimed as your own.

Millennia later, when I offered you my heart of stone,
you etched it with the only word I needed.
You enfleshed me, gave me
ears to hear and a mind to decipher,
a mouth to speak the spirited language
that had bewildered me until that day.
Warm and illuminate me, I pray,
with even one tongue of your holy fire.
By your Spirit, enkindle me kindly
and teach me to speak
words few and true,
incandescent with compassion,
radiant with praise.

This Is My Body

The twelfth step of humility is concerned with the external impression conveyed by those dedicated to monastic life. The humility of their hearts should be apparent by their bodily movements to all who see them. Whether they are at the work of God, at prayer in the oratory, walking about the monastery, in the garden, on a journey or in the fields, wherever they may be, whether sitting, walking, or standing they should be free of any hint of arrogance or pride in their manner or the way they look about them.

(CHAPTER 7, ST. BENEDICT'S RULE)

This is my body, bowing for you,
my face earthward, my gaze on my shoes.
These are my hands, open as wings,
and this is my voice, blending
with a unison of psalmody.
These are my feet, upheld by the firm,
springy certainty of soil,
caressed by the grasses I pass.
The road, compressed, unfurls underfoot.
Its histories of travel
show me the way I should go.

Whatever arrogance I wield as I venture
through my life, relieve me of it.
Help me believe and remember
what is true:
my body is your gift to me;
my pursuits, my prayer to you.

In chapters 8 through 18 of the Rule, St. Benedict outlines the order of psalms and canticles for monastics to sing each day of the year, with seasonal and other variations. Contemporary Benedictine communities normally follow a different order from Benedict's, inspired in part by his comment in Chapter 18 of the Rule: *We have no hesitation in urging that, if any are dissatisfied with the distribution of psalms they should rearrange them in whatever way seems better. . . .*

Despite departures from St. Benedict's recommended order for the singing of psalms and canticles, contemporary Benedictine communities generally practice the traditional *Opus Dei* (Work of God), also known as the Divine Office or Liturgy of the Hours, in keeping with these guidelines from the Rule's sixteenth chapter: *The words of the psalm are: "I have uttered your praises seven times during the day." We shall fulfill that sacred number of seven if at the times of Lauds, Prime, Terce, Sext, None, Vespers, and Compline we perform the duty of our service to God. . . . About the night Vigil that same psalm says: "In the middle of the night I arose to praise you."*

The Curve of Time

In the re-creative dark
of bullfrogs chanting,
of telephones silent in their cradles,
my dreaming shows me where my prayers
are wearing thin.
In your unsleeping mercy,
you summon me to vigils
and I begin again.

Dawn, the lauds hour, mists in gentle stealth
the eastern horizon yellow-blue.
Morning oversees the industries of sparrows,
the slow-jointed stirrings of women and men,
the supple, swift awakenings of children.

According to the westward curve of time,
sun buttresses heaven all day,
then pools, low and golden,
in late afternoon. For this, I give you
vespers-praise, the day's Magnificat-yes
to a promising, embryonic rest.

In compline, I call to you
by candlelight, by cricket talk
and firefly flicker. Holy water droplets
fly, fall on my hair, and send me
to a new, dew-drenched night.

The Labor of Prayer

God's presence to us is never so strong as while we are celebrating the work of God in the oratory.

(CHAPTER 19, ST. BENEDICT'S RULE)

You summon me here for the labor
of prayer, and hum within
the congregation's one, hymning voice.
Antiphons that underscore the themes of grace
frame and reinforce our common praise.

In the unsung pauses between psalms,
my mind stays still, or wanders.
You offer, through both chant and silence,
Spirit-guidance I
may thankfully retrace one day.

To Receive and Reflect

We really must be quite clear that our prayer will be heard, not because of the eloquence and length of all we have to say, but because of the heartfelt repentance and openness of our hearts to the Lord whom we approach. Our prayer should, therefore, be free from all other preoccupations and it should normally be short. . . .

(CHAPTER 20, ST. BENEDICT'S RULE)

Like a rung gong, a singing bowl
whose lingering note calls a meditator's mind
to awareness,
your clean silence welcomes me
to lay my worries at your feet
and rest, wide awake, in your company.

Scrub away the residue of yesterday.
Polish the bell of my soul
to a high shine. Ready me
to receive and quite clearly
reflect your simple light.

Another Name for Servant

Deans should be chosen from among the community. . . . Their office will be to take care of the needs of the groups of ten placed under them and to do so in accordance with God's commandments and the instructions of their superior. They must be selected for their suitability in character and gifts so that the abbot or abbess may, without anxiety, share some responsibilities with them. . . . If any of the deans are affected by some breath of pride which lays them open to adverse criticism, they should be corrected once or twice or even three times. *(CHAPTER 21, ST. BENEDICT'S RULE)*

Rabbi, you call leaders
not to lord it over others
but to answer their needs.
In your economy, *leader*
is another name for a servant
guided by the breath of Spirit,
wisdom's sigh.

The breath of pride blows hard
wherever human beings gather,
even for the purpose of worshiping you.
Inflated,
we hyperventilate,
get dizzy and stupid and have to sit down,
catch a true breath,
begin again.

If you find me filling my lungs to capacity
with an air of grandiosity, teach me,
the way a newborn baby must learn,
to breathe,
not in gulps and gasps
but in even, humble inhalations
and sighs.

I Practice Resurrection

All should be prepared to rise immediately without any delay as soon as the signal to get up is given. . . . In the morning, as they are getting up for the work of God, they should quietly give encouragement to those who are sleepy and given to making excuses for being late.

(CHAPTER 22, ST. BENEDICT'S RULE)

Light penetrates the blinds
(the moon having deferred to the sun)
and the code-world of my dreams
slips away for the day.

I practice resurrection, getting up
though getting up seems, at best,
improbable. Especially reluctant
are these creaking knees, and this brain,
muffled by the gauzy residues of sleep.
Primitive, pre-caffeinated,
close to original innocence,
I'm groggy as Lazarus
and you're alive, Jesus,
repeating, repeating,
Get up.

In chapters 23 through 30 of the Rule, St. Benedict elaborates on the theme of community members' faults and their punishment. Contemporary monastic communities interpret or adapt these guidelines with characteristically Benedictine flexibility and historical sensitivity, seeking always the Rule's enduring relevance without resorting to unhelpful anachronism. In a comparable spirit, I have chosen to limit my prayers inspired by these chapters to the one that follows.

The Friction of Difference

If an individual in the community is defiant, disobedient, proud, or given to murmuring or in any other way set in opposition to the holy Rule and contemptuous of traditions of the seniors, then we should follow the precept of our Lord. Such a one should be warned once and then twice in private by seniors. (CHAPTER 23, ST. BENEDICT'S RULE)

Part of me will always be anarchic.
I worry for the ones who perpetually
tiptoe, too timid ever to test a boundary,
or probe a prohibition.
Where is their lives' electricity,
the friction of difference,
the tension, innovation, creativity?

Jesus, you respect my questions.
You asked them, yourself,

whenever you healed on the Sabbath
or partied with the riff-raff.
Every woman you ever talked with,
the Samaritans and Magdalenes, learned
that God blesses our transgressions
when they're the only way
love's law can be fulfilled. Jesus,
govern my conscience.
Teach me to distinguish
childish defiance from justified dissent.
Help me dismantle, according to your gospel,
policies that silence and dispirit your people.

And should I rebel only for the sake
of disruption, reverting from adult
to adolescent, correct me.
Send me compassionate advisors,
and by their wise counsel, return me
to the heart of your community.

Each Sacramental Thing

All the utensils of the monastery and in fact everything that belongs to the monastery should be cared for as though they were sacred vessels of the altar.

(CHAPTER 31, ST. BENEDICT'S RULE)

candle flame swaying, gassy on its wick
coffee—muggy, sending up steam
plastic pen, plaster bell, potted cactus
the radio, a blue-spined book, a book of matches
each sacramental thing remains itself and means you, too
who are luminous
dark as espresso or ink
swollen with potential song
succulent yet cautionary
eager, patient, all-beginning
all-response

Share and Repair

Anyone who is negligent in dealing with the monastery property or allows it to deteriorate must be corrected with a view to improvement.

(CHAPTER 32, ST. BENEDICT'S RULE)

Deathless. Everlasting. Forever and ever, amen.
I pepper my prayers with these words
for your timelessness, but I confess:
I'm unacquainted with eternity.
I count birthdays, watch clocks,
measure the meanings of my finite life.

Like every other citizen of my time and place,
I was trained to consume and dispose.
Swaddled since infancy in throwaway clothes,
I over-value innovation.
When I sense my goods have gone out of fashion,
I turn them to trash, then scrounge
for the credit or cash to upgrade.

You intervene through a voice
undiminished by fifteen centuries.
Benedict urges me to take back my garbage,
to care for my property, share and repair it.
Like an heirloom, preserve it.
Make it last, like a legacy.

Unlearning Possession

Following the practice of the early church described in Acts, everything in the monastery should be held in common and no one should think of claiming personal ownership of anything. (CHAPTER 33, ST. BENEDICT'S RULE)

Neither deprivation nor excess,
poverty nor privilege,
in your household.
Even the sheets on "my" bed,
the water flowing from the shower head,
belong to us all and to none of us
but you, who entrust everything to our use.

When I was a toddler,
I seized on the covetous power
of "mine."
But faithfulness requires the slow
unlearning of possession:
to do more than say to a neighbor,
"what's mine is yours."
Remind me what's "mine"
is on loan from you,
and teach me to practice sacred economics:
meeting needs, breaking even, making do.

Of Fairness and Care

This principle from Scripture should be established in the monastery, namely that distribution was made to each in accordance with their needs.

(CHAPTER 34, ST. BENEDICT'S RULE)

For each mouth, sufficient cooked fish,
and a few morsels more for the ravenous.
Bread enough for everyone, and tough tasty crusts
for the teething young.
Water and wine in clay cups,
mugs of milk for the frail.
Dark, oily olives, and dates, sticky as candy, for all.
These suit and complete me. I'm sated, grateful,
capable of fairness and care. Is anybody still hungry?
I've been given provisions to spare.

Kitchen Eucharist

Everyone in the community should take turns serving in the kitchen and at table. No one should be exonerated from kitchen duty except in the case of sickness or the call of some important business for the monastery, because serving each other in this way has the great merit of fostering charity. . . . One hour before the time of a meal those serving in the kitchen should each receive a drink and some bread in addition to their regular portion. This will help them to serve the community at mealtime without stress and without murmuring about their lot.

(CHAPTER 35, ST. BENEDICT'S RULE)

A biscuit saved from breakfast
washed down by two gulps of juice
makes a quick, kitchen Eucharist.
Casserole for a choir bakes in the great glass pan,
noodles and gravy gently bubbling their prayers.
I peer into the oven's hot, orange mouth,
and my eyeglass lenses cloud over with steam.
Quilt-mittened, I remove the evening's hot concoction:
an offering to you of savory incense,
your gift to us of sustenance.

Your Broken Body

The care of those who are sick in the community is an absolute priority which must rank before every other requirement so that there may be no doubt that it is Christ who is truly served in them.

(CHAPTER 36, ST. BENEDICT'S RULE)

Eternally alive, daily ailing Christ,
the difficult gift of resurrection
enfleshes you in us, the ill, the old,
in human conditions from which early death
could not exempt you.
You are Christ with arthritis,
anemic Christ transfused by fortified blood from a bag.
Christ, your sacred heart is enlarged,
your lungs, functioning at half-capacity,
each inadequate breath an irreversible reminder
of decades of unfiltered cigarettes.

Christ, you bear our fragility, our foolishness,
our long, helpless habits, all our medical histories.
Your white robes are our hospital-issue pajamas,
your spear-wound, the indignity of our catheters.
The corridors beyond our doors are bright, long, and loud.
Our shallow, fitful sleep is yours,
our fear and boredom, too. Crucified Christ,
have mercy. Risen Christ, have mercy.
Come back to earth and have mercy on us,
your broken body: we're you.

An Armful of Light

Human nature is drawn to tender concern for those in the two extremes of age and youth, but the authority of the Rule should reinforce this natural instinct.

(CHAPTER 37, ST. BENEDICT'S RULE)

Marveling at your miniature features,
I coo over you
and your seamless, iridescent skin.
You mirror my own original innocence:
I once was an infant,
flawless, otherworldly as you.

But all memory of my fresh-from-God self
lies locked in the whorls of my grown-up brain.
When I slept and suckled, was I, like you,
purely prayerful? Diapered Christ,
was I, too, an armful of light?

Two Hungers

There should always be reading for the community during meal times. *(CHAPTER 38, ST. BENEDICT'S RULE)*

I have two hungers:
one, of the belly,
a second, of the mind.
I'm tempted to feed my mouth

unmindfully, to finish off my fast,
fast, and fill myself until
that deeper emptiness, the longing
to know you, is muffled,
if not fulfilled.

My animal body contains
an aspiring soul. Help me
as I chew and swallow,
to read the world for your signs,
to taste and see that you are good,
better than bread, meatier than meat,
sweeter, more to be savored, than food.

Two-Footed and Striving

Everyone should abstain completely from eating the flesh of four-footed animals except, of course, the sick whose strength needs building up.

(CHAPTER 39, ST. BENEDICT'S RULE)

One cat
perches on a windowsill, contemplating sparrows,
while another lounges, tongue-grooming her paws.
Predatory, curious, meticulous,
carnivorous yet sinless, these beasts
have much to teach me of watchfulness,
sufficiency. They leap, they sleep,
they inhabit their lives so matter-of-factly,

they seem to know who they are.
Do they need my prayers?
Or do I, two-footed and striving,
stuttering and stumbling, need theirs?

Spirits

. . . having due regard for the weakness of those whose health is not robust, perhaps a half-measure of wine every day should suffice for each member of the community. . . . Let us at least agree that we should drink in moderation and not till we are full. (CHAPTER 40, ST. BENEDICT'S RULE)

I love, therefore
I love a drunk.
I know no one exempt
from alcohol's pervasive charms
and harms.
Throw your arms, saving God,
around me. Teach me how
to love my alcoholic.
Spirits pass through his lips
to his belly, through his skin,
to his kin. All of us who love him
become intoxicated.
I may be sober as a Puritan,
but my dedication to just one addict
pulls me like an undertow
into the deceptive sea of his disease.

Awash in its cold devilries, seasick
and powerless, all I can pray is, *save us.*
Or merely, *save me.*

The Lean Path

From Pentecost throughout the whole summer on Wednesday and Friday they should normally fast until mid-afternoon, provided that they are not working out in the fields or exposed to an excessively hot summer. . . . The principle is that the superior should manage everything so prudently that the saving work of grace may be accomplished in the community and whatever duties the community undertakes they may be carried out without any excuse for murmuring. (CHAPTER 41, ST. BENEDICT'S RULE)

Whether the murmuring you hear
is the involuntary grumbling of my unfed belly,
or the willful complaining of my otherwise empty mouth,
it's not prayer. Grousing has power
to drown out the deep, wordless sighs
of your Spirit inside me.
Strengthen me to withstand my body's
arbitrary cravings. Help me not to speak
the ingratitude that burns on my tongue.

The longer I live under your sustaining gaze,
the more reliant I become on you
to see me through my shallow hungers,

to call me away from all the self-indulgences
arrayed before me, buffet-style.
Show me to the lean path of patience and restraint.
Teach me to pray my way to breakfast,
a simple, gratefully broken fast.

Catching Your Breath

Silence should be sought at all times by monks and nuns and this is especially important for them at night time.

(CHAPTER 42, ST. BENEDICT'S RULE)

I hear the twilight falling, soft as linen over the earth.
I hear the soil drinking its dew.
I hear my own ear receiving you,
the shell of my flesh catching your breath,
its concealed canal and deeper drum humming
in answer to your prayer for the world,
more music than word. It sings inside me.
My silence, at its finest, harmonizes.

Hurry To This Work

When the time comes for one of the divine offices to begin, as soon as the signal is heard, everyone must set aside whatever they may have in hand and hurry as fast as possible to the oratory. . . . The essential point is that nothing should be accounted more important than the work of God.

(CHAPTER 43, SAINT BENEDICT'S RULE)

A singular, demanding note,
the bell of disciplined devotion,
intervenes in the day. Didn't I already pray?
What more is there to say, so soon?

You. Your name,
the ancient phrases of the faithful
fill my mouth. My mind,
the most defiant part of me,
lingers over what I set aside
to hurry to this work.
To aspire to ceaseless prayer requires me
to live as though you were my highest priority.
I say you are, yet I resist, internally preoccupied
while singing psalms so seemingly sincerely.

Help me. I'm a master of little but self-division:
my body is present, apparently prayerful;
my attention, anywhere but here.
Find me and remind me whose I am,
what my deepest joy is,
why I need much practice
as well as your forgiveness.

Chapters 44 through 46 of the Rule focus on the themes of penance and reconciliation for monastics whose errors have led to their excommunication from the community, or to a milder form of punishment. Despite Benedict's moderate approach relative to the norms of his own time, twenty-first-century readers will tend to find aspects of these chapters severe and anachronistic, especially where the punishment of children is concerned. Chapter 46, however, concludes with a remarkably compassionate directive for adults: "*. . . if the cause of wrongdoing lies in a sinful secret of conscience, it should be revealed only to the superior or one of those in the community with recognized spiritual experience and understanding, who will know the way to the healing of their own wounds and those of others without exposing them in public.*"

A Story of Redemption

Battered Jesus, liberating Christ,
despite your unjust injuries, bone-deep and raw,
you rose up, unbound by bitterness,
and spoke my name. I heard it plainly.
You meant to bless and free me.

Once, I'd been violated, hurt so profoundly
I fled for my life
into a strange and sudden solitude.
I wrapped my bruised being in protective bandages
until I was thoroughly swaddled.
No daylight could reach me, no prayer
escape my insulated lips.
Yet you must have caught some muffled moan of mine,
because you came to me, the clay of your grave
still clinging to your hair, and called my name
until I couldn't deny what I'd heard.

In cautious answer, I unfurled
my self-made cocoon, to stand before you,
blinking, tender-fleshed, startled by the freshness
of the dawn air. Until just then,
gauzy dark had enveloped me, and my wounds
had thickened into scars.
You laid your own nail-marked hands on them
and told me, *These will always be yours.*
Your torn-and-healed skin will tell a story
of redemption. Your body will bear witness
to sin endured, and finally forgiven.

A Secret I Contain

Only those . . . should come forward to sing and read who have the ability to fulfill this role in a way which is helpful to others. *(CHAPTER 47, ST. BENEDICT'S RULE)*

Today, let my service be silence,
my ministry, listening.
Let my voice remain
a secret I contain.
Help me keep a vocal fast,
and be led by others,
fed by their hymnody and Scripture.
Open me sufficiently
to welcome sung wisdom pointing your way,
to embody antiphons and canticles
singing your praise.

Reading This Day

Idleness is the enemy of the soul. Therefore all the community must be occupied at definite times in manual labor and at other times in lectio divina.

(CHAPTER 48, ST. BENEDICT'S RULE)

Morning opens like a book of fresh-written Scripture.
You dwell, quiet but lively in its pages,
ready to whisper to my heart's ear,
to be answered by my hands' work.

It seems simpler than it is—
reading this day for your resonances.
You press me to attend
reverently to everything,
even the tedium: the dishes.

Cereal bowl with a sweet milk residue,
and coffee cup, faintly stained, sit in the sink,
resplendent as sacramental vessels. If only
I will see them as such,
and wash them with a mindful,
genuflecting touch.

Search Me

There can be no doubt that monastic life should always have a Lenten character about it, but there are not many today who have the strength for that. Therefore we urge that all in the monastery during these holy days of Lent should look carefully at the integrity of their lives and get rid in this holy season of any thoughtless compromises which may have crept in at other times. . . . Thus each one of us may have something beyond the normal obligations of monastic life to offer freely to the Lord with the joy of the Holy Spirit. . . .

(CHAPTER 49, ST. BENEDICT'S RULE)

Search me, penetrating Spirit.
Drag my depths for the sunken
accumulations of my life.
Retrieve it all:
the old, unhealed wounds,
the memories I've tried to keep
from you, who alone
can remedy and soothe.
Receive my sacrifice
of grudges, the sludge of unforgiveness,
the slights I horde like old green pennies,
the pettiness I practice to protect myself
from pain. I offer you the worthless cache
of my spirit's cuts and bruises, the elaborate
self-deceptions that have long-outlived their use.
Take what you find in the sodden sea chest
of my mind, and show it all to me.
Let me see what I've submerged:
what I ought to salvage,
what it's time to purge.

Ever Available

Those whose work takes them some distance from the monastery so that they cannot manage to get to the oratory at the right times for prayer must kneel with profound reverence for the Lord and perform the work of God at their place of work. (CHAPTER 50, ST. BENEDICT'S RULE)

I know you're here
ever available,
ever receptive to my prayer.
Not you but I am the busy one
with the crowded calendar,
inclined to fit you in mainly when
I have a cancellation, as though
your mercy were my last priority,
a rare luxury.

My preoccupied hours and days
go by, and I relegate you to a corner of my mind
until I feel free to grant you full attention.
But I have no fullness to offer.
I give you a hollow stare and feel I've become
a passing acquaintance of my Creator.
I speak a few stiff sentences,
then lapse into embarrassed silence.

There—if I dare to linger in the discomfort—
dwells the potential for the prayer I need,
an honest encounter between my hectic heart
and your uncomplicated patience.
I face you for the thousandth time and find

I'm a beginner,
a sinner not in some spectacular act of evil,
but in a collection of petty forgettings
that summon my repentance
in remembrance of you.

Gradually, a miracle flows into me, a stilling
and filling of my anxious, empty self.
Now calmed, now capable of reverence,
I pour my awareness into you,
only to receive much more than I give:
the prayer I pray, the very life I live.

Go Home Hungry

Any who are sent on an errand which will allow them to return to the monastery on the same day must not eat outside, in spite of pressing invitations whatever their source, unless the superior has approved this.

(CHAPTER 51, ST. BENEDICT'S RULE)

Thoroughfares are lined with signs
urging me to eat here, eat fast, eat cheap.
The breeze is fat with scents:
fried potatoes, grilled meat.
It's all designed to cultivate
hurried hunger, speedy satisfaction.
I've consumed these hot, soggy meals
served in a paper box, and marveled

at their tastelessness, the great, bland
caloric heft of it all.

The psalmist called,
O taste and see that God is good.
Such poetry could not have been inspired
by billboards for overweight food.
The most prayerful answer I can offer
is to go home hungry,
peel an orange,
chop a heart of celery,
devil a dozen undecorated eggs.

The Chapel Unchanged

The oratory must be simply a place of prayer, as the name itself implies, and it must not be used for any other activities at all nor as a place for storage of any kind. . . . Anyone who . . . wants to pray privately may very simply go into the oratory and pray secretly, not in a loud voice but with tears of devotion that come from the heart.

(CHAPTER 52, ST. BENEDICT'S RULE)

The middle of this city
was once the edge of town.
A chapel rose up from hard, gold earth.
A steeple bell rang against a changing sky,
summoning monks, reminding
working people to pray.

Your house is now surrounded
by a hundred humming avenues,
but the chapel remains unchanged. It's still
a cool, hallowed hall, tall and buttressed,
blessedly singular in purpose.

With Us

Any guest who happens to arrive at the monastery should be received just as we would receive Christ himself, because he promised that on the last day he will say: I was a stranger and you welcomed me. . . . The greatest care should be taken to give a warm reception to the poor and to pilgrims, because it is in them above all others that Christ is welcomed.

(CHAPTER 53, ST. BENEDICT'S RULE)

In the airport, we're required to remove our shoes.
I stand, stocking-footed, arms outstretched,
praying that the ground be holy.

We're briefed
on oxygen procedures, emergency exits,
then settle into this, our airborne, uppermost room.
I wonder, Jesus:
are you ascending with us,
or has Security detained you?

The Treasure

. . . it will be for the superior, after agreeing to the reception of the gift, to decide who in the community should receive the gift and, if it is not the one to whom it was sent, that should not give rise to recriminations lest the devil be given an opportunity. (CHAPTER 54, ST. BENEDICT'S RULE)

Talents and callings don't come gift-wrapped,
but like presents, sometimes they come by surprise,
dazzling and devilish in their capacity
to inspire both gratitude and rivalry.
Great Giver, I pray
for the ones whose abilities sit,
unopened, unnoticed, like some small Christmas gift
buried beneath bigger, brighter packages.

For the unsung musician toiling at a day job in a cubicle,
a keyboard numerical and noiseless before him
while the music in his mind goes silent, I pray.
For the woman whose half-remembered wounds
bind and gag her like a kidnapper waiting for a ransom,
I pray the revelation will come
that the treasure lies within her and she is free
to discover her giftedness and be happy, at last.

We, your star-struck people, obsessed by celebrities
on whom we project so much of our beauty,
page through slick weeklies and wonder why it isn't *me*
inspiring the envy of the neighbors and hot pursuits
by paparazzi. Could it be because you made us life-sized,
talented yet fallible and mortal?

Could it be every one of us is gifted,
a humble, human miracle?

More Than I Needed

. . . the superior must provide all members of the community with whatever they really need, that is: cowl, tunic, sandals, shoes, belt, knife, stylus, needle, handkerchief, and writing tablets. Every excuse about what individuals need will thus be removed. There is one saying, however, from the Acts of the Apostles which the superior must always bear in mind, namely that proper provision was made according to the needs of each. (CHAPTER 55, ST. BENEDICT'S RULE)

In wooded mountains, at a meadow's edge,
I heard your Spirit rushing, hushed,
from one stand of aspen to another.
Hummingbirds buzzed by and fussed.
Silver-green aspen leaves shimmered above
white, papery trunks knotted with dark eyes.
Meadow grasses, nibbled down by elk,
lay low beneath the sky's uncomplicated blue.
Swallows dove, chasing insects, air currents, each other.
Calm and high, a raven circled and cruised,
waiting, perhaps, for someone to die—
maybe me. I wouldn't have minded.
You'd given me more than I needed, and a pen
for writing in praise of the day.

Refectory Gestures

The superior's table should always be with the guests and pilgrims. (CHAPTER 56, ST. BENEDICT'S RULE)

Itinerant, tentative, unacquainted with the customs,
I showed up at the monastery scarcely aware
it was you I sought. I found
companions in my search, seekers in the pews
nearly outnumbering the sisters in the choir,
learning the liturgy as I did,
by sincere imitation, error, and correction.

I wondered: would I ever know sufficiently
the rhythms of the antiphons and canticles
to sing them unselfconsciously,
to sense your presence in the chanting of the psalms
and the silences between?

Then came a dinner invitation, a glimpse into a cloister
less mysterious than I had imagined.
Off a hallway hung with portraits of past prioresses,
an inviting, sunlit dining room smelled of pot roast.
The tinkle of a hand bell at the prioress's table,
and her spoken "peace"—both blessing and command—
quieted all table talk. She introduced me by name
and looked my way across invisible aromas of gravy and
coffee.

Surely everyone was hungry, but the welcome came unhurried,
warm and true as a cup of soup.
The prioress led us in praising you, then nudged me

to the buffet, urging me to fill my plate first.
By these gracious refectory gestures, my eyes were opened,
and I, the sisters' grateful, honored visitor, recognized you
in the breaking of the dinner rolls, the savoring of dessert.

The Work of Their Hands

If there are any in the community with creative gifts, they should use them in their workshops with proper humility. . . . If any product of the workshops is to be sold, those responsible for the sale must be careful to avoid any dishonest practice. . . . What is asked by the monastery should be somewhat lower than the price demanded by secular workshops so that God may be glorified in everything.

(CHAPTER 57, ST. BENEDICT'S RULE)

Monastic sisters who labor and reside side-by-side
in a Clyde, Missouri, house
cook, cure, slice, and market scented soaps—
lavender-vanilla, oatmeal-spice.
But most of their revenue comes from altar breads,
translucent, sacramental wafers they bake by the thousands
for parishes nationwide.

The Benedictine brothers down the road run a printery shop.
Handpainted icons, some gold-leaved, gaze,
dark-eyed and seemingly remote to the casual customer
who prefers packets of greeting cards and marvels
at the bargains in the monastery gift shop.

"Sometimes it's hard," say the bookkeeper-sister, the
brother-cashier,
"to remember that it's God we seek to glorify by our crafts
and commerce."
They wonder if the monks in Kentucky, famous
for their smelly, mail-order cheeses, boozy fruitcakes,
and prolific, best-selling Merton, find it any easier
to maintain the monastery as a school for the Lord's service,
a sacred, ancient enterprise supported by a modern retail
business.

Jesus, worker of wonders,
bless the artisan and mercantile monks:
the carvers of cutting boards and canners of jam,
California's bee-keeping, honey-bottling Cistercians,
Arizona's contemplative candle-dippers and vestment tailors,
Pennsylvania's Benedictine publisher-prophets.
Jesus, answer the monastics' brief, incisive prayers
for a world consumed by poverty and profiteering.
Help the sisters and brothers keep their practices and prices
fair,
and prosper, O, prosper the work of their hands.

A Place in the Cloister

The entry of postulants into the monastic life should not be made too easy, but we should follow St. John's precept to make trial of the spirits to see if they are from God.

(CHAPTER 58, ST. BENEDICT'S RULE)

In an age when most male monks
have been rendered bald-headed
not by the razor but by years,
and mere smatterings of gray-haired sisters
filter into echoing convent chapels for prayer,
I fear the demise of monastic tradition:
communities living for you, alone.

This era, terrorized and polarized,
aches for sanctuaries, places where "peace"
is not only etched above entryways
but also practiced within.

Sitting, shut-eyed in the monastery chapel,
I lift up to you my worry
that this center of stability I cherish
will die for a lack of new vocations,
and be resurrected as condo complex
for well-heeled tenants with a taste for sacred architecture.
I wonder: should the monks make it easier
for postulants to claim a place in the cloister?

The quiet, vaulted church,
this refuge from the traffic just outside,
suggests an answer, of sorts: you

who are compassionate and patient, ageless and wise,
hear my anxious devotion,
and without a word,
you make me smile.

Parent Us Anew

If parents who are from the nobility want to offer to God in the monastery one of their children, who is too young to take personal responsibility, they should draw up a document . . . and, as they make the offering, wrap the document with the child's hand in the altar cloth. . . . Poor people may make the offering of a child in the same way.

(CHAPTER 59, ST. BENEDICT'S RULE)

In French, the child is called *le donné,* the given.
In Hebrew, Hannah names the son she begged of you,
Samuel, "the borrowed one," then gives him up
to live in the temple under the priest's care and tutelage.
Unimaginable, it seems today—
a parent parting with a wanted child.
Monasteries long ago abandoned the practice of taking
them in.
To my generation of scandalized skeptics,
the biblical story is just as unthinkable: Eli the priest,
sleeping unsupervised beside the boy Samuel.
Yet it was precisely there
that you called and called again Samuel's name.
So many call you "Father." You are our tender Abba,

"Papa" to the young Jesus, who terrified his parents
when he stayed behind with teachers in his Abba's house.
Jesus came to trust you so deeply
that later, he refused to resist his crucifiers.
Survivors of unspeakable yet infamous abuse
understand how Jesus hung there,
helpless, sacrificial, thirsting for mercy.

Parent us anew, Abba God.
Take us back, not to the womb, but to the heart
of your compassion, your protective embrace.
Call us and call us again by our true names.
Teach us love and limits—
when and to whom to say no, or yes.

All Believers

An ordained priest who asks to be received into the monastery should not be accepted too quickly. If, however, he shows real perseverance in his request, he must understand that, if accepted, he will be bound to observe the full discipline of the Rule and may expect no relaxations.

(CHAPTER 60, ST. BENEDICT'S RULE)

A thousand years after Benedict lived, a monk named
Martin Luther called for the priesthood of all believers.
He sought the abolition of even Benedictine monasteries,
whose Rule was as humbling to the mighty
as Luther's own 95 theses.

Half a millennium past the Reformation,
I worship you, Jesus, under the influence
of Benedict, Hildegard, Luther, John Calvin,
and a great cloud of lesser-known, everyday saints
whose lives illustrate this gospel truth:
whatever may be one's cultural rank,
it's reversed in your realm,
where the lowly ascend,
and the powerful aren't, in the end.

Passing Through

Monks or nuns on a pilgrimage from far away, who come to the monastery asking to be received as guests, should be received as long as they wish to stay, provided that they are content with the local style of life they encounter and cause no disturbance in the monastery by any excess in personal behavior. *(CHAPTER 61, ST. BENEDICT'S RULE)*

At turns, my eyes were dazzled, then soothed,
by Kentucky's curvaceous green hills.
I rounded a bend
and a stark stone cathedral confronted me
as if to confirm that everything I'd driven past—
Louisville's urban machinations,
bourbon distilleries reeking of corn mash,
tobacco fields, yard sales—
belonged eternally to you,
and even the oldest, most steadfast monks

of this abbey, Gethsemani,
were merely passing through.

I'd arrived for a weeklong sojourn
to do what monastic pilgrims do:
at the alarm clock's merciless predawn beeping,
awaken
and shuffle to the chapel for the liturgy of vigils.

Later, I'd wrap my devotional hands
around a Melamine mug of weak coffee
and pray into my oatmeal.
In the silence of the common dining room,
I'd get a feel for this paradoxically
shared and solitary life.

I'd stare through the window
of the guesthouse library, at the stone words
GOD ALONE
overarching the cloister garden
I was prohibited to enter.
I *was* permitted to venture
into the sunny cemetery and pause before
Father Louis Merton's unremarkable gravestone.
I'd glance around and sneak into the woods for a glimpse
of his cinderblock hermitage.
The word carved in a plaque beside its screen door
both chastened and blessed me: *Shalom*.
God, I was a silly spiritual tourist, but then
naughty curiosity was a virtue Merton admired.
On my way back to the chapel for none,
a Trappist on a golf cart buzzed past me

with two passengers,
pilgrims from farther away than I'd traveled.
Their saffron robes fluttered
and framed the driver's black-on-white.
We were all in a hurry to pray.
We all waved.

Humbling Privilege

When ordained a monk must be careful to avoid a spirit of self-importance or pride and he must avoid taking on himself any duties to which the abbot has not assigned him. . . . His ordination to the priesthood should be no occasion for him to be forgetful of obedience and the obligations of the Rule, but he must more and more direct the growth of his spiritual life towards the Lord.

(CHAPTER 62, ST. BENEDICT'S RULE)

When the warm hands
were laid upon me, and my knees
pressed into the floor, absorbing its stony cool,
the scent of molten beeswax
mingled with the clean spice of celebratory carnations,
and I knew
your Spirit had befallen me.
I was ordained
to the humbling privileges of priesthood:
finger painting a spikenard oil cross
on the forehead of a woman

skeletal with multiple sclerosis;
lifting a plastic shot glass of grape juice
to the lips of a man whose heart failure
seemed only to deepen his capacity for love.
And the lonelier tasks: locking up the church
after everyone else has gone home;
looking up and seeing, with ordinary eyes,
the ceiling, or at best, the stars,
and hoping, believing in my heart
you live and move beyond them,
yet here below them, too.

Before the Infant

Age must never be the deciding factor in community order just as it was that Samuel and Daniel judged their elders when they were still only boys.

(CHAPTER 63, ST. BENEDICT'S RULE)

Despite the arthritis in some of our joints,
we all fall to our knees
before the infant in the carrier.
Her sleeping eyes, crescent-creases tinged periwinkle,
don't twitch. She's dreamless,
and we are brought to a heightened wakefulness,
a soft awe, by her small serenity.
We cluster like magi and gaze
into her exquisite face.
I can walk, talk, and do all the things grownups do,

but mostly I gawk, speechless and still,
aware that you're here,
certain the baby is you.

Called to Serve

The abbot or abbess, once established in office, must often think about the demands made on them by the burden they have undertaken and consider also to whom they will have to give an account of their stewardship. They must understand that the call of their office is not to exercise power over those who are their subjects but to serve and help them in their needs. . . . They should always bear their own frailty in mind and remember not to crush the bruised reed. (CHAPTER 64, ST. BENEDICT'S RULE)

She stood before me, formidable, too fleshy
to be called a "reed." But bruised she was, and told me why.
An old story, new in her experience:
she'd been overpowered by the very person
called to serve and help her. Two tears
slid down her cheeks while she blinked back the rest,
and withheld, I could tell, some of her story's details.
But she gave me her wounded and passionate self,
and I give you that difficult gift in this prayer.
Hear her, heal her through me and any other soul
who has a long time to listen and a life
tenderized by compassion.

Teach leaders the difference between
authority rooted in wisdom,
and arrogance, frailty's tempting
but foolish, brutish disguise.

Part of the Garden

It is best in the interests of preserving peace and charity that the authority for the whole administration of the monastery should rest with the abbot or abbess. . . . It is best that everything should be organized through deans according to the wishes of the superior.

(CHAPTER 65, ST. BENEDICT'S RULE)

At the point of a floppy over-flourishing, a loose, gaudy
excess
beyond all proportion,
you pruned me.

Now I stand strong, centered and simple,
rooted,
part of the garden,
not the garden itself, nor the gardener.

It's hard
to accept the necessity
of such humility
when it feels so good to bloom wild, run riot.

I once was a wildflower: random, impulsive,
but you have long since cultivated me
to grow slowly, in concert with a community,
not confusing my few sturdy leaves and bright blossoms
for the whole, labyrinthine flower bed
or the garden's central tree.

Working, Worshiping

The monastery itself should be constructed so as to include within its bounds all the facilities which will be needed, that is water, a mill, a garden, and workshops for various crafts. There will be no need for monks and nuns to wander outside which is far from good for their monastic development. (CHAPTER 66, ST. BENEDICT'S RULE)

Water flows, purified and modern, from faucets,
shower heads, sprinklers in the orange grove's soil,
hoses snaked amid the monastery roses.

Instead of an old-fashioned mill there's a superstore
where all the sisters' groceries are bought in one stop.
But still, in a workshop traditionally cloistered,
custom vestments hang, newly sewn by sister-tailors,
awaiting priestly wearers and the proper season:
ordinary green,
pentecostal red, penitential purple,
resurrection white.
Year-round, for decades, for life,

vowed women live and work
in this microcosmic training ground for heaven.
You leaven them through liturgy,
lectio, labor, and leisure.
They stay
through jubilees silver and gold,
working, worshiping,
preparing by prayer for a world
without end.

Your Protective Reach

Those who are sent on a journey should commend themselves to the prayers of all the community as well as of the superior and, at the last prayer of the work of God in the oratory there should always be a memento of all who may be absent. (CHAPTER 67, ST. BENEDICT'S RULE)

In summertime especially,
the migratory nature of your mercies
emerges. Your people hit the road,
fly the skies, ride the waters in boats—
however grand—small enough to be swallowed,
traceless, in an hour.

Wanderlust,
or vacationers' simpler escapism
test the boundaries of your protective reach
and find it has no boundaries.

Whether I fasten a tank to my back and sink
into the sleek, muffled world of deep fishes,
or strap an illumined helmet to my head
and crawl underground amid incremental
mineral formations,

always you have gotten there first—
a maverick explorer who allows me
my navigational mistakes
and makes the most of them,
watching over me, leading me
to some serendipity:

the unrepeatable play of this
particular sunlight on the sea floor,
or the prismic flashing in my eyes
of seeming color and light, despite
the cave's unmitigated darkness.

Until the Impossible

. . . if the burden of [a] task appears to be completely beyond the strength of the monk or nun to whom it was assigned, then there should be no question of a rebellious or proud rejection, but it would be quite right to choose a good opportunity and point out gently to the superior the reasons for thinking that the task is really impossible.

(CHAPTER 68, ST. BENEDICT'S RULE)

Rarely have you reached me
in any way but gently.

I can count two occasions, maybe three,
when you moved mightily in my life,
and then only briefly, just long enough
to seize my attention
as a flame seizes a moth's.

Once you had me, you moved
so gradually you nearly bored me.
You held me as amber holds an ant,
in a slow, gold embrace, an envelopment
that seems accidental,
and certainly deadly,
but over time grows beautiful
until the impossible has happened:

you've broken what I long believed
were your own rules.
The world is changed.
The bug's become the jewel.

All the Solidarity I Need

Great care must be taken to avoid any tendency for one of the community to take the side of and try to protect another. . . . *(CHAPTER 69, ST. BENEDICT'S RULE)*

When she ran to my rescue
she turned against my enemy.
At first I welcomed her advocacy: at last
someone understood the injustice that had hurt me.
Or did she need a victim with whom to identify,
a scapegoat with whom she could vicariously die?

Already you have accomplished
all the solidarity I need.
You, the only Christ, have risen
above disastrous human loyalties
to teach us to love
not by way of unexamined compulsion
but with risky compassion
that may require suffering with a companion,
but rarely to the point of a partnership in martyrdom.

Black-and-Blue Souls

. . . anyone who flares up immoderately against children must be subjected to the discipline of the Rule, for it is written in Scripture; do not do to another what you would be unwilling to suffer yourself. (CHAPTER 70, ST. BENEDICT'S RULE)

I know too many black-and-blue souls,
violated girls and battered boys
hiding in the memories of women and men—
your grown children, injured generations
with spirits stunted and bodies haunted
by adults who once overpowered them.

In your tender and redemptive name,
I reject violent doctrine. Atonement's been won
not by the mutilation of your Son,
but by your resurrecting mercy,
which surpasses all destruction.

Cast your kind gaze
into each survivor's scarred mind.
Find there, under decades of enforced forgetting,
childhood trauma and its terrifying tools:
a belt in the shadows,
a hand on the mouth,
secrecy, threats, shifting rules.
The body of Christ
bleeds internally.
Only your eyes, luminous and accepting,
can bring healing light to the wounds.

A Holy Mutuality

Obedience is of such value that it should be shown not only to the superior but all members of the community should be obedient to each other in the sure knowledge that this way of obedience is the one that will take them straight to God.

(CHAPTER 71, ST. BENEDICT'S RULE)

Obedience is not made of servitude,
but attentiveness. Prayer is best expressed
not by giving you to-do lists, but in listening.
At my best, I listen well for your whisper
in the words and behavior
of my sisters and brothers,
the blessed, peculiar creatures
who people my life.

One is driven to give so richly
he risks depleting his strength.
Another is already emptied
by her lover's greed, disguised as need.
She calls her slavishness "obedience,"
but you don't. Within that word
is balance, a holy mutuality
imagined in Benedict's century,
still relevant in ours.

In asking for obedience,
you call us all to paradoxical fulfillment.
It comes when we answer one another's
fair requirements. Obeying in your name
decent purposes not my own, I may seem

to postpone or sacrifice my happiness,
but your timely providence and all-sufficient peace
are what I seek for others
who seek the same for me.

The Daylight of Your Spirit

It is easy to recognize the bitter spirit of wickedness which creates a barrier to God's grace and opens the way to the evil of hell. But equally there is a good spirit which frees us from evil ways and brings us closer to God and eternal life. It is this latter spirit that all who follow the monastic way of life should strive to cultivate, spurred on by fervent love. . . . They should value nothing whatever above Christ himself and may he bring us all together to eternal life.

(CHAPTER 72, ST. BENEDICT'S RULE)

I remember the church's earthen walls,
protective and warm.
Like your everlasting arms,
they held us,
but couldn't keep our bitterness at bay.
Fear had infected us, and territoriality,
and all the small poisons of character
to which human beings fall prey.

The church walls became an ironic bulwark
impeding your grace. I remember
walking from the parking lot to the prayer garden,

the sun on my face, the cold in my heart,
as though you'd been barred from the church,
forgotten, or locked in some car.

But here you are. It's always here
you are. Not you but I needed release,
to be freed from my interior shadows,
the Sheol in my soul, then led
back to the daylight of your Spirit,
the welcome of your household.

To Begin

Whoever you may be, then, in your eagerness to reach your Father's home in heaven, be faithful with Christ's help to this small Rule which is only a beginning. Starting from there you may in the end aim at the greater heights of monastic teaching and virtue . . . and with God's help you will then be able to reach those heights yourself. Amen.

(CHAPTER 73, ST. BENEDICT'S RULE)

You make me eager
as an alphabet
to break ranks
and tell a story,
say a prayer.
You make me
eager as a street
to show the way
to wheels and feet,
eager as a fire for wind to burn,
as a river for skies
to deepen its blues,
for a life to baptize.
You make me
eager as breath to be taken
and given, eager as death
to find you in heaven.
You make me eager
to come to the end,
eager as Easter
to begin.

Acknowledgments

My sincere thanks go to Abbot Patrick Barry, Father Anselm Cramer, and Liam Kelly of Ampleforth Abbey, and to Gracewing, distributor of Abbot Barry's translation of St. Benedict's Rule, which was instrumental in the composition of this book.

I am deeply grateful to the Benedictine Sisters of Perpetual Adoration for welcoming me into their home and their life. Especially to Sister Lenora Black, OSB, Director of Tucson's oblates and Editor of *Spirit & Life* magazine, for her friendship and hospitality, both personal and editorial, I offer my heartfelt thanks.

To Melanie Supan Groseta, oblate OSB, my dear friend in whose Alpine, Arizona, cabin I composed several of these meditations, and to all of Arizona's oblates of St. Benedict, I thank you for sharing your oblation with me.

To Jon Sweeney of Paraclete Press, who not only blessed me with good news on the feast day of St. Benedict, but also lent his wise editorial insights to this work, I offer my gratitude. My thanks also extend to other members of the Paraclete staff: Lillian Miao, Jennifer Lynch, Danielle Bushnell, Sister Mercy, and others whose careful efforts contributed to the book's completion.

To my loved ones, and to friends and associates whose faithfulness teaches me the ways of God, I am grateful for your love, support, and companionship.

I extend special thanks to: every member of the Srubas family; all of my in-laws and their dear partners; Rev. Susan Reggin; Rev. Dr. Rose Carol Taul; Jean Bronson; Cassandra Fraley; Rev. Ren and Florence Davis; the Pearce family; the

Dellaria family; Rev. Melani Longoni; Greg Foraker; Rev. Dr. Fran Buss; Rev. Patricia Kilcullen; Rev. Dr. Lib Caldwell; Jane Chilcott; Dr. Annick Safken; the Casey Home for Girls; my colleagues throughout Presbytery de Cristo and the Hesychia School for Spiritual Directors; all participants in that ministry of beloved memory called "Prayerful Practices"; and all the other beautiful souls—too numerous to name—with whom I've had the privilege of praying over the years.

To Ken (again): with all that I am and all that I have, I love and thank you.

About Paraclete Press

Who We Are

Paraclete Press is an ecumenical publisher of books on Christian spirituality for people of all denominations and backgrounds.

We publish books that represent the wide spectrum of Christian belief and practice—Catholic, Orthodox, and Protestant.

We market our books primarily through booksellers; we are what is called a "trade" publisher, which means that we like it best when readers buy our books from booksellers, our partners in successfully reaching as wide an audience as possible.

Paraclete Press is the publishing arm of the Community of Jesus, an ecumenical monastic community in the Benedictine tradition. We are uniquely positioned in the marketplace without connection to a large corporation or conglomerate and with informal relationships to many branches and denominations of faith. We focus on publishing a diversity of thoughts and perspectives—the fruit of our diversity as a company.

What We Are Doing

Paraclete Press is publishing books that show the diversity and depth of what it means to be Christian. We publish books that reflect the Christian experience across many cultures, time periods, and houses of worship.

We publish books about spiritual practice, history, ideas, customs, and rituals, and books that nourish the vibrant life of the church.

We have several different series of books within Paraclete Press, including the bestselling Living Library series of modernized classic texts, A Voice from the Monastery—giving voice to men and women monastics on what it means to live a spiritual life today, and Many Mansions—for exploring the riches of the world's religious traditions and discovering how other faiths inform Christian thought and practice.

Other Benedictine Titles Available from Paraclete Press

A timely biography of the original St. Benedict, patron saint of Europe, father of Western monasticism, and inspiration to our pope

Man of Blessing: *A Life of St. Benedict*
Carmen Acevedo Butcher
176 pages; one map
ISBN: 1-55725-485-0
$21.95 Hardcover

Towards the close of the fifth century, in a time of war and want, Benedict left behind a life of privilege to live in a cave and learn how to be silent. There, he also learned how to walk the way of truth and be God's friend. This monk and abbot aimed to establish and nurture community, cultivate the wilderness, and feed the poor. He also left us his famous Rule, seventy-three short chapters that are the foundation for Western monasticism and remain a spiritual classic.

You don't have to live in a monastery in order to live like a monk

How to Be a Monastic and Not Leave Your Day Job
An Invitation to Oblate Life
Br. Benet Tvedten
128 pages
ISBN: 1-55725-449-4
$14.95 Trade Paper

Most oblates are ordinary lay people from various Christian traditions.What connects them together is The Rule of St. Benedict. And in today's hectic, changing world, being an oblate offers a rich spiritual connection to the stability and wisdom of The Rule, as well as an established monastic community. This essential guide explains how—even if you live and work in "the world"—you can still live and practice your spirituality like a monk.

Available from most booksellers or through Paraclete Press:
www.paracletepress.com; 1-800-451-5006.
Try your local bookstore first.